The A[...]
Wit[...]

To Alan a class-mate who helped me through this. You will allways be in my thoughts and [...]

Tom

Thomas Westmoreland

chipmunkapublishing

the mental health publisher

The Agony Within

All rights reserved, no part of this publication may be reproduced by any means, electronic, mechanical photocopying, documentary, film or in any other format without prior written permission of the publisher.

Published by
Chipmunkapublishing
PO Box 6872
Brentwood
Essex CM13 1ZT
United Kingdom

http://www.chipmunkapublishing.com

Copyright © Thomas Westmoreland 2011

Edited by Lucy Lythgoe

ISBN   978-1-84991-668-4

Chipmunkapublishing gratefully acknowledge the support of Arts Council England.

Thomas Westmoreland

The names in this book have been changed to protect the privacy of the individuals involved.

The Agony Within

Preface

Some people may relate to what I have written in this book. Perhaps you have experienced the same agony or a relative or loved one has. Others might be unable to relate to this book and say *so what*? But in crowded pubs, shops or office spaces, there will be a handful of people or even more who will have faced something similar or be about to face it. However, until you have suffered it is very difficult to understand. I hope that this book may help both sides.

For me, the title of this book, explains it all. The agony to which I refer is worrying. It can be so destructive. You actually reach a point where you worry because you are not worrying. You start to find that you will recheck items such as whether you locked a door, not once or twice but eight or nine times or whether you switched an appliance off at the mains. You may walk away, but then you go backwards and then forward not trusting yourself, which can impact on your self-esteem and will create a spiral of worry and low trust in yourself. You might ask how I have reached this day and to be honest, I do not know. During the time it is happening, you do not know that it is taking place. I think at some point we all have experienced what I label as *dark thoughts*, but the issue is how you control them. I must admit that when I had those feelings there was no fear, only after did this come. With insight it is so easy to look back and now for me, I think it has always been there. It is this insight that I want to bring to you, in the pages that follow.

This book is about my journey from my early days to adulthood, the highs and the lows. I hope that you enjoy this book and it will give you an introduction to my perspective of *The Agony Within*.

Acknowledgments

I would like to thank my wife Debra and my daughters Rose and Roberta, for being there. I am grateful for both Gordon and Ken for being available to both talk and listen and to Arthur for being on the end of that phone. With regard to my counsellor Jill; words are not enough.

In addition, I would like to thank Julia Everitt for voluntarily reading through my original notes and offering to edit them, so they made sense in English. Julia assisted to develop my notes and she edited them into a book format for me, which was then suitable for publication. Julia has acted as my voluntary editor and representative and I am thankful for her drive, enthusiasm and belief in the words that I wrote and in what we would like to achieve in raising awareness.

I would also like to thank Chipmunka for publishing what I have written and bringing this book to the readers, with the view to helping others and reducing stigma.

Finally I would like to thank Dr. Chaudry, Wendy, Ray, Tony and Anita who gave me that break I needed, in the form of employment.

The Agony Within

Table of Contents

Preface
Acknowledgments
Table Of Contents
Chapter One: Why?
Chapter Two: Growing Up
Chapter Three: Alone In Hospital
Chapter Four: Dad
Chapter Five: Early Days At Work
Chapter Six: Working Hard
Chapter Seven: Mum
Chapter Eight: Death
Chapter Nine: Working Too Hard
Chapter Ten: Feeling Unwell
Chapter Eleven: Belief
Chapter Twelve: Luck
Chapter Thirteen: Getting Better
Chapter Fourteen: Getting Back To Work
Chapter Fifteen: Being Judged
Chapter Sixteen: It Never Goes Away
Chapter Seventeen: Dark Thoughts And Death
Chapter Eighteen: Here And Now
Chapter Nineteen: Family

The Agony Within

Chapter One: Why?

I originally started to write about my feelings and experiences to enable me, in part, to come to terms with what I call 'the agony within'. It was only after talking to Julia my colleague, who offered to read my notes and afterwards suggested that she would edit them into a book format for me and assist me to share my story, that I decided to go ahead and have them compiled into this book. However, the intention was never to aim for a complete story about myself or write an autobiography. The plan was to keep it short and thus it is a brief look at 'the agony within'. However, Julia has assisted me to elaborate on my original notes and write more, as we have progressed through the editing of my notes into this book, hopefully with the result of a more rounded story for the reader.

Overall, this is my interpretation of the way that I felt and the help that I received. I have no doubt that this was quite an upheaval for my family. It is one of the hardest things to attempt to explain. I hope if you do read this and you feel similar, that it will highlight that you are not alone and are not stupid, daft or crazy. This is what I believe and I know that there is help out there.

I have found that since I started to write towards the creation of this book and talk to people about it and what I have experienced, that there are many individuals out there that feel the same or have been touched by the way that I felt during this process. I believe that if you can talk about it, then this helps, but you also need someone to support you. I understand that there are different levels of what individuals will experience, but if my story helps one person, then I feel that it is a job well done. I am not a doctor. My current job is a caretaker and I love it.

The one thing that I will say is that I will never forget 'the agony within'.

Chapter Two: Growing up

I actually enjoyed the place where I grew up, with my brother and two sisters. I was quite lucky that it was the time that you could leave your house doors open and feel safe. If you wanted a drink or a sandwich then you were given one: dripping, sugar on bread and of course condensed milk on bread. How yummy. Like many people, I had two sorts of aunties, the ones that you were related to and the ones that were not, but they were my mum's friends, who we would call Auntie. You could always call on them if you wanted a drink or a sandwich; they were just nice people. In terms of relations, I think that I had one special aunt, my dad's sister, who lived in Brighton Hove; we spent many a holiday down there and they were good times.

With my mates I had some fun, which included the game *kick the can*, which we played for hours. The amount of games that we played was numerous, including kite flying, marbles and conkers. The summer holidays seemed to be hot and long, with crashes of thunder that would wake the dead, although we were always told, it was 'angels rolling the barrels across the sky'. During the holidays we would ask Mum to make us a sandwich, normally it consisted of jam and would be wrapped in the paper from the loaf of bread. We would play over the fields and far away for the day, train spotting or just going to the woods and climbing trees. We played hide and seek and many more games. At the bottom end of the estate was a part that we called the *swamp*, a place just filled with dragon flies, various plants, frogs, newts, stickle backs and different species.

We also had a large pool on a different part of the estate but a few children had lost their lives there. Mum and

Dad always warned us that we should never go in there. However, we would swim in the shallow part. The council put a paddling pool right next to the lake, which seemed a bit stupid; two vast concrete mounds together. In the winter when it snowed, we would get a plastic bag and sit in it and slide down the mounds and we tried not to end up in the lake. One time my two sisters and I walked across the frozen lake, which was scary. We made it without going through, but if Mum and Dad had found out, there would have been trouble.

However, from an early age I can remember worrying which ranged from how I was doing at school to how I looked or who might want to be my friend. I do not think there was a day which passed when going to school that I would not worry about something, including my clothes or the way I looked. I think that I was very conscious of the way I looked from my glasses to my hair cut. I am not sure if everyone felt like this, but I knew I did. Was I insecure? I do not know. I never spoke to my mum and dad about the way that I felt, all I knew was that my head felt full. Sometimes I probably spent more time worrying about what other people thought, than concentrating on my school work. I never felt that school helped me in achieving the type of work that I wanted. I wish I had the help that school children receive today. It could be argued that we all worry, the difference for me is the extent of the worry and how it can affect your life.

When I was growing up, I had to contend with many things. I was trying to fit in with those around me, which was made all the more difficult by superstitions. As far as I can remember it was Mum that was behind all the superstitions, from not bringing green into the house, to spilling salt, all of which can play quite a part in your life. I might be walking down the road and would be told that if I stood on the cracks in the pavement, then someone would die. If I spilt salt, I had to throw it over my left shoulder, into the eyes of the devil. I could not take a green stick into the house or break a mirror, for the thought of the seven years bad luck that it would bring. These are just a selection, but there were many more.

When I was younger, one of the things that I loved to do was just to lie on the back lawn of my mum and dad's house, look up at the sky and make pictures out of the clouds and feel the warmth of the sun. I think at times, I just liked to be on my own. I felt great solace in this. In my life, I have had a few special friends, which I am grateful for. However, one of the biggest battles was my desire to be accepted and liked by everyone around me. We know that in the real world this does not happen, there are always some people with whom we do not connect. To me this made no difference; I needed to be liked. I had some great friends on the estate, but there were arguments, which I never liked and I always felt sensitive towards them. I just wanted to be friends with everyone and hated it when arguments happened. I did not have the strength like some. I can remember falling out with some mates on the estate and it was one group against the other. All I ever wanted was for everyone to be friends, but we know that this does not always happen.

Reading this book, you might ask what relevance this has with 'the agony within'. Well they may not be the cause, but they did not help. I find myself being very protective towards my own children, not putting any pressure on them regarding some of those old foolish and stupid superstitions. We try to guide them through life and yes to have feelings, but not let those feelings ruin their childhood or to take them into adult life; I think there is a fine line.

The Agony Within

Chapter Three: Alone in hospital

As a youngster, under eight, one of the worst times I spent in hospital, was when I had Scarlet Fever. I am still not sure what this was, but I recall I was isolated in a room, which has stuck in my mind for years. Mum and Dad would come to visit me; you would not believe the joy that I felt when they arrived. There I was stuck in this room, hour after hour and just the sight of the food they served, made you feel sick, and particularly after the Matron insisted you ate it all.

There was nothing nice about being in hospital. There I sat with Dad, just chatting away, and then he said that he had to go. That was it, I did not want him to go and I welled up. I pleaded with my dad not to go. He stayed for a short while, but then the final bell went and he said he had to leave. I asked him not to and felt the tears begin. I saw that Dad was uncomfortable with this. I was now full of tears and I jumped out of bed. Dad put me back in bed. I told him that I wanted to go home, but he reassured me that I would be home soon. The matron or a nurse came and told Dad he had to go. As the door shut behind him and I saw him go, I decided that I would not stop there. I leapt out off the bed, opened the door and when I saw Dad in the corridor, I shouted and ran towards him, yelling and crying. Dad gave me the biggest hug, but the nurses intervened and ushered me back to the room. I thought the room was horrible and I cried myself to sleep. Was it worry or fear? It could have been a bit of both. I was never too sure how long I would be in hospital. At this young age I cannot remember anyone telling me what was happening. I feel it is very important to understand even at such a young age. Later in life, I discovered that this affected my dad and upset him somewhat.

On another occasion I had to go into hospital for an ingrown toenail. As I lay there an elderly gentleman next to me explained how he had started with an ingrown toenail and how it had turned to Gangrene. He was now to have his leg amputated at the knee. I am not sure how this happened, but this put fear into me. Whilst I waited for my operation, these conversations with the elderly gentleman did scare me somewhat, just the fear of not knowing the outcome. Yes I was worried. In the ward where I was located after my operation, there were young children and babies. I could hear them crying and I felt so sorry for them; all I wanted to do was to go to them and make sure that they were comfortable. This memory of them crying and being upset has always stayed with me, which you may think is odd.

One time I was knocked off my motorcycle and ended up with a punctured lung. I woke up to find myself lying in the road and had been covered by a young lady. She told me to relax, but I found myself short of breath and felt tired. An ambulance arrived, into which I was lifted and then it seemed to be moving at speed. Someone asked me my name and tried to keep me awake. We entered the hospital and the staff members were hurrying around me and they cut off both my jacket and shirt. I did not feel frightened at all, but quite relaxed, although I was not sure why, maybe I felt in safe hands.

I still felt out of breath, which was from my punctured lung. They entered a thin metal tube into my chest, which did not hurt, but I was hooked up to what looked like a demy-john. I was told to do breathing exercises, which was to repair my lung. Debra, my wife walked in and her eyes welled up. She was so upset but I reassured her that I would be fine and that I was in the best place. I had ripped some muscles in my shoulder and had to be visited by a very determined physiotherapist, although you can understand why they are trying to improve your health. My wife visited me at lunchtime and in the evening, which I felt was great. However, the doctors came around the ward and informed me that I was ready to go home the next day and I could not wait.

The following morning I felt that something was amiss, as I felt cold. The nurses were good; they brought more blankets and extra beside because I felt so cold. I was told that the doctor would see me shortly and it turned out that I had penicillin poisoning as I was apparently allergic to it. My wife arrived and I gave her the good news that I would remain in hospital, which then for me was the best place to be.

So my opinion of hospitals had completely changed. As I became older I found that being in hospital was quite a safe place. What else could happen in hospital? There is no one to criticise you, all you had to do is sit back and get well. It is quite strange really as now I find hospitals quite relaxing with doctors and nurses there telling me what I should be doing. This I suppose is what I have always wanted.

The Agony Within

Chapter Four: Dad

Love or hate the working men's clubs, but on the estate where I grew up, there were two of them. As I grew older I began to hate the place. One was situated only a few hundred yards behind the house, over a short copse. It played a big part in my dad's life, but then it was the place for all the miners to meet. It was quite funny, you had all the locals in one spot, the Geordies in another, which my dad was one, and then the Scottish in another. We went there with Mum and Dad and were given a bottle of pop and a bag of crisps, which was quite a novelty at first. Then there were the Christmas parties, what child would not be happy with that? There were some good acts on the stage, but then again that was the era when the working men's club were a big interest, according to Dad.

I have a couple of photographs of Dad, one of him playing football for the club and the other when he was a club committee member and thus captured during their ritual photograph. Dad filled all the posts: treasurer, committee man, secretary, although treasurer was his favourite, as maths was his best subject. He would not let anyone deceive him. In my teenage years, I remember some chap complaining to me because I said that if you have a boss who pays a fair wage, then he deserves the profits that he makes, because he was the one taking the risk; for some reason this was not well received.

I think the club did take over my dad's life to our detriment, but I am not sure. As a child I saw that my dad went to the club Saturday lunch time, back for dinner which we always had at two, then he went to bed until about five-thirty, then he returned to the club. He did the same on Sunday. I am not sure if this happened every Sunday, but it seemed like it did.

I think Dad was at home for Saturday tea but we always knew that he would be going out that night. However, Saturday tea used to be great. Mum would make pies, such as egg and bacon and I loved them. We sometimes had crusty batches with bacon that you have never tasted before, not like the spit and water filled type you get today. We also had pints of milk which had the cream at the top. Then there would be the chap in the van that would come up the street selling fresh bread and cakes. The cakes would be on a shelf, which would be pulled from the side of the van, not that we had one all the time. The ice cream seller would also come up the street and on a rare occasion we would be sent out to get a dish of ice cream.

Regarding the club, I and a few mates were collecting around Bonfire Night asking people if they had a 'penny for the guy'. We had made a stuffed guy and would ask people that passed by, if they would chuck a penny in. We would sing something like *remember, remember the fifth of November, if you have not got a penny, a half penny will do, if you have not got a half penny then God bless you*. We were stood between the shop and the club, but when Dad came out of the club he was absolutely furious. He said we were begging and there was no place for it. I had never seen him so annoyed. We think someone in the club must have wound him up about it. We scarpered, and I went home and waited for Dad to come back from the pub. I was sure I would be told off, but nothing happened. I cannot say that the club was bad; it just was not for me. The thought of seeing the same people, sitting in the same seats at the same time, on the same days, conjures the word *boring*. Towards the end of my dad's life, I asked him if he had any regrets in anything that he had been involved with. He said he wished that he had not become involved with the club so much. However I feel it is perhaps no good looking back. Someone once told me, that it must have seemed that it was the right thing to do, at the time.

I loved my dad, but I think that I missed him because of his work and the time that he spent at the club. There was no doubt that he worked hard to provide for us all, but sometimes I think we needed more. My granddad, Dad's father was a nice chap, although Dad never spoke too much about him. I would go to Granddad's house at dinner, probably because Mum and Dad could not afford the school dinner money. He never really talked that much. The one thing that I do remember about him was the size of his hands, they where massive. I never felt that close to him, but then I was never close to either of my grandparents. However, I was to learn that at times, he was not always as nice as I thought. He was a miner; he worked hard and drank hard, sometimes losing his wages at the pub. He turned up at our house once on a Sunday afternoon in a taxi; Dad and Mum were not happy. What the relationship was, I am not sure, Dad always said he did not want a family life for us like he had, but he would not say any more about it.

I occasionally wish that Dad had spent a bit more time with me, as we did not talk that much, not until later in his life. However the blame cannot rest with one person. Should I have spoken to Dad more? I think it was a cycle in those days, where you went to school, you left to acquire a job and then met someone whom you would marry. If anything has shown more in life, then I was quite normal. It is perhaps the actions taken to acquire them. In terms of 'the agony within', I suppose I always felt that others were doing better than me and perhaps it was not quite like that.

The Agony Within

Chapter Five: Early days at work

Whilst at school I had a Saturday job at a butcher's shop; which was a job share with my friend Gordon, who I had known since primary school. It was Gordon's job at first, but I was asked to step in when he could not make it. Whilst there I met Bill whom unbeknown to me, would become my employer, at some point in my life.

I also tried my hand as a paper delivery boy, but found this hard work. I seemed to walk miles delivering the local paper, this was every evening and also on a Sunday. In addition the school sports teacher informed me that I had to choose between the school football team and their training sessions or the paper round. The choice was easy; for the small amount I received for the paper round and how hard it was, the football team appealed. However I kept the Saturday job in the butchers until I left school.

I do wish that my dad had told me which route to take and regret that Dad did not tell me to stay on at school, but I suppose we could all say that. However, I needed to be told what to do, it had always been that way and I still needed it then. I am not sure if I had stayed on at school if this would have changed the way I have always felt. I think that I left school for the wrong reasons; I just went with the flow. I believe that I did not have the confidence to make my own mind up, which has always been problematic. Why did my dad not give me the advice? I have thought about it quite often. Did I give the impression that I was confident and knew what I wanted? I do not think so. During this chapter and the others about my working life, you will discover that I had many jobs. Did my lack of direction influence the amount of jobs which I had? I am not sure. I enjoyed most of the jobs that I had, I think it was money that was driving me just to make sure that we could pay the bills at home, no different to anyone else I suppose, but I cannot say that they were the jobs that I really wanted to do.

As I said I needed to be told what to do and so I wish that Dad had spoken to me about work and what it would be like when I left school. I cannot say that he gave me much advice; I seem to have been just left to get on my merry way. I really wanted to be a PT Instructor in the army, but when I went to join up; they told me to come back in a year when my acne had cleared up. I did hear one of them say that my eyes were no good. That did knock my confidence, and by the time the year was over, I was doing a job elsewhere and I suppose I felt safe, and feeling safe is all I have ever wanted. I suppose that I myself did not know what I wanted and I think the only real advice that Dad gave me about work, was that he did not want me to go down the 'pit' (coalmine). If I had received more help at school I could have been something else, but I suppose everyone could say that. I think that looking back, 'the agony within' has always been with me.

When I started to work, I think my ethics were that you never progressed anywhere unless you worked hard. A friend helped me to get my first job, at a place where he and his mum worked. It was called *Skins* and the work involved *Tanning* and *Turing*. *Tanning* involved taking the sheep skins and turning them into rugs and coats, whilst *Turing* was the process of making suede, from some of the skins. It was awful and I can remember the stink! I lasted there about two weeks and when I walked in my mum and dad's house and told my dad that I could not work there any longer, my dad's response equated to "what will you do next?"

Two days later I had an interview in a factory which manufactured ladies' underwear and tights. The warehouse manager who interviewed me was such an arrogant person; I immediately took a dislike to him. The questions he asked were mainly mathematical, which I still do not understand. He asked me what I expected and I told him I would like to make progress in a career at the factory. I was given the job and Dad was very pleased, also about how I handled myself. I started work in the warehouse the following Monday. I was situated at this bench with a young man, in his twenties. The job involved putting tights into boxes and I stood there for about four hours, doing just that. The young man that I was working with was just a bit too friendly for me.

Later I had a chat with one of the ladies on the shop floor and asked how she was. It was just a bit of small talk in which she asked me what I wanted to achieve, both out of life and my job there. I told her that I did not want to work in a warehouse all my life. At this point she told me that I should get used to it because all the lads that had held the job previously, had all believed there was a chance of promotion, but this was never the case. I approached the manager and asked him about promotion and he replied that I should not have unreachable ideas and that he was the one to do the management. He informed me, in an unpleasant manner to return to the warehouse and fill boxes. At that point I told him that I was not prepared to be spoken to in that manner and I walked out.

My third job was at *Tetro* in the home and wear department, acquired after an interview that went well and during which I was told that I would get a pay rise, if I worked well. I looked forward to this job and the female workers on the shop floor were good work colleagues. I was taken to a warehouse, which was a bit odd, as it was a caged area in a warehouse. When the manager showed it to me my heart sank; it was such a mess, there were boxes of stock everywhere that needed sorting out. I thought let me see what I can do. The department manager said that if I could sort the warehouse, I would receive a wage rise. I did not need to be told twice. Over about eight months I worked hard and even implemented a stock card system, which achieved the approval of the female shop floor workers. I even made the floor shine; it was time to ask for a pay rise, from my £4.25 per week to approximately £5.00 per week. However when I visited the manager who really commended my work, he stated that the pay rise was out of his control. I wondered if I asked for too much or was wrong to ask. All the self-doubt started to flood in. I had worked six days a week, from the day I started, including Thursdays, which was half day closing. I had a chat with Dad and decided that I was not going to work like that for £4.25 a week.

It did not take long to find another job, with a firm called *Larry's*, in the butchery department. The manager was called Michael, but was known as Mick. There were two of us who would have a trial for the position and at the end of the trial, I was lucky enough to be employed as a butchery apprentice. Peter another trainee was a nice lad and we had a good relationship, but they had a scam going and it was discovered that he was involved in the scam (I wondered if this caused him any agony?). I left *Larry's* for a short time to work in one of Bill's shops, whom I mentioned previously that I knew from my Saturday job, whilst at school. However, to be honest I found this job to be a bit too quiet and went back to *Larry's*.

However, one of the things I realised whilst at *Larry's* is that you should never believe the hours that you are told at the start of employment. I was informed that it would be a thirty-six hour week, however, it was more like sixty-six; but it was a job that I loved and I was still conscientious. However, I used to worry what Mick and Peter, my co-worker, thought about me. Even when they told me that I performed a good job, this still was not enough for me. I wanted perfection and whatever level I carried out, I still wanted to improve so to achieve this I secured a manager's job in the *Larry's* store in a Staffordshire town. I used to get up at five to catch a bus at five forty to arrive at work at seven forty. I enjoyed it very much and always thought that it was hard work being employed in a store, but I always gave it my best shot, but again never thought that this was good enough.

I felt lucky when I noticed an advert for a butchery manager at the local Warns. I applied and was awarded the job. The workers were lovely and the store manager was one of the finest men you could ever meet. Despite this, it was still hard work and I felt that I had to prove to everyone, including myself, that I could do the job. Yes I was still worrying and when I look back I think that I was trying too hard to please everyone. I moved from the butchery department to the delicatessen department and again I had to prove to others and myself that I could do the job. Although it was hard work, I believe that I succeeded.

One good thing about Warns and probably the best thing that has happened to me was that I met Debra there, whom I have mentioned briefly before and whom became my wife and we married whilst I worked at Warns. At first Debra would not become my girlfriend until she had confirmed that I was single, because I had been engaged to another girl. After some time I asked her out, but I always wondered if I was good enough for her. There was my own self-doubt and the worrying if we were compatible and at the time no matter what reassurances she gave me, there was always doubt in my mind. When we decided to get married I always felt that I had to prove to her parents that I was good enough. Strangely the person, to whom it meant the most, told me that I had nothing to prove. Mine and Debra's first Christmas together was spoilt as I was exhausted from work, but Debra said that she was just happy to be with me. I had worked twelve hours each day for a month, to ensure we achieved the sale targets. At what cost? You might ask. Perhaps I should have learnt from that. I did not and you will find why if you read on.

Chapter Six: Working hard

I left Warns to work at Crooks a metal cutting factory, which was a change from meat. I heard about the job through my dad who already worked there and thus I worked there with him and I enjoyed it. However, I had to keep my distance, because there were some employees that were suspicious of my employment there so again I had to prove to them and the management, that I was capable. I worked there on two occasions and I was always worried and aware of what people thought of me. I just wanted to be friends with everyone, but at a cost to myself. I realised that this could not happen. I enjoyed my time there and thought it was a great job. I could cycle to work with ease, as I could not drive at the time, which was not a problem, as I felt the job was not that testing.

During my first employment period at Crooks, I had a second job. The appeal was that my uncle used to do some gardening for a butcher and somehow I ended up working there after my daytime job, on a Friday and then all day Saturday. It was great, an old fashioned type of place, that made all their own sausages, pies and cooked meats. If the truth be known I would have worked there for nothing. The chap who owned the business was very nice, but he liked a drink and his mum and dad who were in their eighties and still worked there, were adorable. The father once asked me if I would like to buy the business and I did go to the bank, but they changed my mind. I explained this to the old boy and he offered to lend me the money himself so I could buy his son's shop, but I could not do that. The shop was eventually sold and my employment there ceased.

The Agony Within

I continued my main job at Crooks, until there was an announcement that the factory would be losing a percentage of the workforce, which was dreadful. I was determined that I would do everything within my power to keep my house. Myself and my wife had only been in our house for three years, during which time the interest rate had increased from approximately 8% to 15%. However I was summoned into the office and handed an envelope and basically informed that I would be leaving. It was not a nice experience. As soon as I heard about the potential redundancies, I had been looking for work, but without success. I left the factory on the Friday lunchtime and started the walk home. I was not on my bicycle, for some reason that I cannot recall. As I walked through the town centre, I noticed an advertisement in a shop window for a sales person and I thought I could apply as it could only be advantageous to me, after being served with my immediate redundancy. I entered the store and asked for the manager and I was told to wait.

After twenty minutes I was ushered into the manager's small office and he was of a stocky build, slightly older than me and quite brash with his questions, such as why I wanted to work in a wallpaper stockist. I felt very uncomfortable in his presence. I explained that I had been made redundant only some twenty minutes earlier and that I was far from work shy and thus would do anything within my powers to ensure I could maintain my mortgage payments. I added details of my work experience. The manager informed me that I had the job, which was a relief, although the pay was not brilliant. Afterwards I wondered whether I should be grateful that I had found a job or if I had just jumped into the first job that appeared. I had some odd feelings walking home, which were a mixture of relief and dread; I was pleased but I was apprehensive about working for the manager.

As I began to leave the town centre and make my way home, I heard a car horn. As the car stopped and the driver shouted, I recognised that it was Bill, who asked why I was not at work. When I explained about my redundancy and recently secured wallpaper stockist sales position, Bill asked whether this was the right choice and told me to report to his factory on Monday morning. This was a meat processing factory, which also made sausages and cooked meats for a chain of stores. I could not believe it; I was going back into the butchery business. What a stroke of luck.

It was clear that I had to take action with regard to the wallpaper sales position, which I had acquired and decided to walk back into town. I was feeling very nervous as I entered the shop and asked for the manager. Again I was asked to wait and after some time, the manager arrived and asked what I wanted. When I informed him that I did not want the position, his words where quite clear and I remember them to this day. He said, 'people like you do not want to work'. I thought, how dare he, I have never been afraid of work and always secured employment, as soon as I could. What did he mean? What did I do? My actions were in line with what I was raised to do, which was to have the courtesy to inform people what was happening. What sort of person was I to get a reaction like that? I just could not believe it. I asked him what gave him the right to say that to me. At that point he asked me to leave the store. I felt quite sick about it and after leaving the store I had quite mixed emotions; I was so angry at what he said but I was happy that I had escaped from working there as I had a new job to look forward to.

On the Monday morning I walked into the office at the meat processing factory and Bill was not there. I was very nervous. However then Bill walked in and put me at ease. He introduced me to the rest of the workers and I felt relaxed. I asked Bill about my role and after a moment's thought he replied that I was his assistant. The time spent in this position, as an assistant to the buyer, looking after the stores, whilst still applying my butchery skills, was one of my favourite times at work, as it was very informal. After six months Bill called me into the office to enquire about my progress, to which I replied it was good, but that I wanted to do more. Bill told me quite frankly that the factory would not be there in a number of years. He perhaps sensed that that I needed security, from our previous conversations. Bill asked if I would be interested in a deputy manager's job in a flagship superstore within the chain, which was due to open. At that time I was scared and anxious, but the thought of a new challenge was overwhelming. I would hate it if I was put in the position where I had no job to move to, so I took the job.

When I walked into the flagship superstore it was quite frantic. I was introduced to the majority of the workers. At times when preparing the store for trading, it seemed as if I lived there. What surprised me was the age of the store manager who was employed, especially with regard to the quantity of physical work involved. He was in his late sixties and after the initial pomp and ceremony of the official store opening, he went off sick. I wondered what would happen then. Well within weeks I had gone from a butcher to a deputy store manager, to being a store manager. The work schedule was quite demanding and at times I felt myself becoming excessively affected by it. Incidents arose which I had not experienced before, but I had to deal with them.

There was a push for sales, which felt unachievable without physically dragging people into the store. The staff employed there were good, which was one aspect that motivated me. However I was often at work for up to fourteen hours a day, which eventually affected my marriage, which I will explain shortly, and at times I became anxious whilst working there. An example of this was when the company paid for a free shoppers' bus from various points outside of our store, to take shoppers into the main town. However I could not understand why and became anxious about it, due to the drive for sales. We were instructed to display the bus timetable within and outside the store, but unfortunately at times they were not on clear display for the shoppers. When one of my bosses entered the store and queried the timetable's location, I became angry and informed him how ridiculous it was that they were giving a free bus into town, when there was no guarantee that they would actually shop in our store, before or after they used the bus to town. The head office was located in town and I was called to attend there and was reprimanded. Did I feel really stupid or was it the other way around? I will leave you to decide.

At the time I worked on average twelve hours a day, including supervising the four hour evening shift. They were a good team who would restock the shelves and it was an enjoyable shift. The responsibility for this should have been split, but as the manager was still off sick, it fell between two of us, the warehouse manager and me. However due to circumstances it generally became my responsibility. They employed an ambitious young lad to assist, but there was something odd about him. Again I was called to the head office, situated in town and informed that I had allowed the evening staff to drink on duty. For a moment I wondered what was happening, and then it became clear. I admitted that I had let the female worker have a drink during quiet periods. However someone had made assumptions on the kind of drink. I left the office with my reputation intact. I was informed that I did a good job, which affected me somewhat, and you can imagine what my brain was doing, it was in overdrive. The job was beginning to take its toll on me.

On several occasions the store had been burgled, which could happen day or night, but more at night. I was always the one to be called out. On one occasion it was about 2am and my wife would always take me to the store and wait to see if everything was safe as I could not drive. She did not like me visiting there on my bike. On this occasion I had to wait for the windows to be boarded up, which took until about 4.30am and I had to be back at work for 6am.

Things were beginning to become strained at home, between myself and my wife, as we did not seem to have any time together. All I seemed to do was spend time at the store and all I would talk about was work. This reached a point when my wife told me that I had to make a choice, either I reduced my hours or it was our marriage at stake. The best part I could understand, but my mind was in turmoil as I had to choose between work and my marriage. What daft person would choose work? However if you are a workaholic, then you would choose work. All I ever wanted was to be secure. I visited my boss and informed him that my marriage was at risk due to the pressure of work. It was as if they were not listening. I had to say this more than once.

I think that if it had not been my wife's strength to tell me exactly how she felt, I could have easily carried on working as I had before. I may have tried to give my wife all the excuses why I should have carried on working. I believed that work was such a drug and that nothing could get in the way, even to the point of destroying anything good that was in my life. We could have split up and had a divorce. This thought really shook me up. I believe some people find it difficult to find that work and life balance, which can be exasperated by the fact that to enjoy life and pay bills we need money. However when you have money, the drug of work has captured you. As I mentioned earlier I believe that I was raised with the ethics that you have to work for what you own and not receive something for nothing. There was such turmoil in my mind, when my wife told me how she felt. I did not realize what was taking place and affecting her so much. All she ever wanted was quality time together, which is not too much to ask. Did I have 'the agony within' already? That is a question that I cannot answer. I believe that if my wife had not had that strength to tell me her thoughts, then circumstances might have been very different today.

At work I was eventually given the choice of managing a small store and I moved there. This I loved but over time the company would pinch staff to work in the flagship superstore, especially when the economy was struggling. The small store staff members made a good team and I enjoyed working there, but history repeated itself and again I was working all hours and the job began to take over again.

After some time, I was informed that my old job at *Crooks*, from which I was made redundant, was available due to the fact that orders had increased. I felt that I needed a change or it might have been that the money was better. I went for the interview and secured the job, but unknown to me after being there for some weeks there had been some rumblings about my employment. The union man had recommended that I should not have the job and it was because I told him a few home truths when I left there previously and I believe he held a grudge and used his position to action. This played on my mind for some time and I felt quite sick and anxious about it. Was this part of 'the agony within'? Luckily I had a strong boss, who told them that it was my job. I never felt comfortable whilst I was there and I was always having to watch what I did and would be thinking about what could happen next. The money and the overtime were good, but it did not stop me getting a second job. Was I a workaholic? I had recently passed my driving test and I would leave home at six-thirty in the morning to go to *Crooks* and then leave there at 5pm and then travel a further 20 miles. I would start my second job, as soon as I arrived there. I do not think that I have ever been afraid of hard work, but sometimes I wonder if I might have been addicted or obsessed, which I am not sure is the sort of thing that you would admit to.

At *Crooks* we became aware that we would be informed that half of the metal cutting factory would be relocated up north and that many of us would be made redundant. I thought that I was lucky because a director from one of the suppliers, a company called *Butts*, had asked if I would like a job at his company. I had to meet the managing director which I did and I passed successfully. However, I wish I had known then what I do now and I would not have taken the position. Whilst there I passed on some of my expertise to the rest of the workforce and the company acquired a very healthy contract. The workers, when I first arrived there, were very suspicious of any new employees and thus I tried my best to have smooth relations with them. I worked there for twelve months for half of their wages, in the hope that I would achieve a contract with the company. However, it seemed that I was fighting a losing battle with most of the shop floor workers, just to be accepted. It was an eighty mile round trip, each day to work and coincided with the time that Debra and I had started a family. When our first daughter Rosie was born we needed two cars. With all this, once my redundancy was spent, we had unfortunately accrued some debt.

My employer *Butts* had taken over another company which meant they needed three employees to transfer to a regular night shift. Yes, I was open to this option, but I had to negotiate with the company regarding my contract. Luckily I received the equivalent wage to the other employees for the night shift, but it was like I had started a new job and I had to get to know the two others that I worked with. They were great; I found Arthur to be much like me, as he just wanted to get the job done. Derek was also a nice chap, but not a very good supervisor, I think he had his own agenda and wanted to be in senior management, but was not thought of as such. Arthur and I would spark off one another and we would just go faster and faster, we just loved it. I think that the way we worked was like a drug and gave us such an adrenalin rush. We worked right to a point that some workers from the other shifts did not like the amount of work that we produced. It was quoted at one point that we did as much in one and a half shifts and the others did in three and when this became common knowledge, we were not liked.

Sadly the employees on the night shift including myself, always had to carefully watch what we did, so we were not criticised. We never seemed to receive information with regard to work procedures or if there was news, we would be the last to know. Most of the workers were friendly enough on their own, but together you would not turn your back on them. I think they were afraid of losing their jobs and would stop at nothing to make sure that they were looked after; it was a bit sad really. At times I believed that the management did not really help and that they sometimes instigated rumours, to keep us all on guard.

However I stayed on the night shift at *Butts* for nine years, until various changes took place. During this time both of my parents suffered ill health and passed away, which is very relevant to 'the agony within'. Therefore I want to talk about this, before we return to the story at *Butts*.

Chapter Seven: Mum

As I mentioned, during my time at *Butts*, I lost both of my parents and I feel this is an appropriate point to talk a bit about my mum, and also the time that she spent caring for my dad. However, before I start this chapter, I want to remind you that I am one of four children and that we all had our own perspective on what we thought about Mum. What is written here is mine.

Mum always worked hard through her life. First she was employed in a munitions factory, then as a cleaner and also within an old people's home. As I write this, I can see her sitting by the coal fire knitting and burning her legs with the heat. At times she must have found it tough bringing up four children. She would always amaze me with the great cooked dinners she produced on such a small cooker. We had one every night except Saturday, then it would be pie or bacon. As a parent now we know how testing it can be so to have two girls and two boys she did well. I loved my mum immensely. I do recall Mum chasing me once, with a cane, when I was about ten. I may have been a bit cheeky towards her. I reached the foot of the stairs and I said, 'you will not get me', but she did. Looking back at some of the pictures of Mum when she was younger, I can see why Dad fell for her.

When Dad became incapacitated, Mum took the role of carer, which would have had an impact on her. Recently I found a small book stored in with some old vinyl records that were passed to me from Mum and Dad, which I have kept in my loft, always meaning to look at them. The front cover of the book has a handwritten label which stated 'day weight and B.P. book' (blood pressure). I imagine that due to the fact that Dad was so poorly Mum must have kept a record for the doctor or hospital. Not only had Mum logged his weight but after the first page, she had started to put comments in the book too. Why she did this I will never know, but after reading the comments I think Mum must have been feeling Dad's pain.

One of the comments stated;

> 'She was quite pleased with him (Nurse) but still says he still does not feel well? Had a break down Saturday; Night sent for our eldest son Thomas (which is me); Dad was asking for him. Son Thomas stayed for an hour until he was calmed down – still not well'.

For me I cannot remember this. Had I blocked this out? That is something that I cannot say. It is strange how your mind will let you remember some things and not others.

Another stated;

> 'Thomas (son) took his dad to the local club. Not well tonight. Vomiting. Bed at eight o'clock.'

This one I do remember. I thought that my dad could do with a change from being in the house, just for a short while. It would also allow Mum a short respite. Although it was intended to be just for an hour, it never lasted that long. I am not sure if Dad should have been drinking, but at that moment in time he felt like a pint. We were sitting and chatting in the working men's club, but Dad could only manage half of the pint. I did not push him to drink the rest. I am not sure how long we stayed there, but on the way home Dad was violently sick. We reached home and Mum was not surprised. Was the creation of these notes in this book, Mum's way of release, to show me that she loved my dad? If I had found this book when I was poorly, I am not sure how I would have handled it. Now I see it as a short journal (notes even) and it makes me feel proud of Mum and Dad; as opposed to sadness.

Another quote states:

> 'Hospital phoned. They will be coming today. No one came. No blood sample taken. Still nobody came to see him. He is very poorly, in bed 8 o'clock, could not get warm, not much better this morning, very low in himself. He seems to think that nobody can do anything for him. I wish he could get help.'

I now wonder whether Mum and Dad were suffering from 'the agony within'. Was I too busy in my own life to understand what was happening to them? Should we have talked more? This I will never know. I believe that sometimes we see 'the agony within' but we do not understand what is happening to us or others, and we need to try and recognise the signs earlier.

Was Mum being tested? The time period that Mum completed the diary over was nearly a year. This must have been a daily worry for them both. Where Mum wished for help, I wonder to what sort of help she refers? I believe that we need to assist families, doctors, employers to try and recognise when someone needs help and not think that they are just 'losing the plot' or are beyond assistance or unable to be helped. Comments such as *pull yourself together, get a grip, get over it;* do not help. How many times have you heard this? How many times have you used these terms? I can tell you that anyone with 'the agony within' does not want to hear this, or will not understand why anyone would say these terms. I believe that they are so insulting to anyone who themselves do not understand what is happening to them. What is needed is for someone to try and understand what we are going through without insults.

How does someone begin to 'pull themselves together' when their mind is in so much turmoil? I was very lucky in that the saying 'get over it' was never used when I was ill. All that people want who are suffering with 'the agony within' is for others to just try to understand. Yes it will be hard. My oldest sister tried hard to understand and wanted some answers, but I could not give her any answers. I was struggling myself to understand, so if you know or think that someone is going through 'the agony within', please think before you speak. I do believe that we require more understanding. Depression is bad enough, as is anxiety, but both together are quite destroying. Just because an individual cannot see what is going on, does not make it easy. We do need to try to develop more understanding on this subject. It is perhaps that 'the agony within' is a scary subject.

Back to Mum's notes, one stated:

> 'He had a very bad heart attack Saturday night at 9pm. Did not want to see a doctor. Gave him medicine and put him to bed half an hour later. Not well this morning. I do not know what to do next.'

This highlights the turmoil that Mum must have been going through at this point, which makes me feel incredibly sad. However, I never heard Mum moan about Dad; she may have done, but not to my knowledge. I wish at that moment in time that I understood what they were both going through. At the time, if we visited, Mum would say that Dad was having an off day, but he would get through. Dad himself would say that he was okay. Why could I not see through this? Did I know how bad he was and just tried to put it in the back of my mind? Perhaps I did not want to hear that Dad was so ill? I think Mum was strong whilst she was looking after Dad, but to a degree part of Mum died with Dad; some of her inner strength had gone. Mum had filled in that book for over a year and was committed to it. Perhaps it was some sort of release. At times, there is different handwriting in the book, which I believe is from healthcare professionals. They perhaps saw how much the book meant to my mum.

It does sound as if Dad's physical health started to affect him mentally. I believe that when you feel physically ill this puts added pressure on the way that you feel mentally and this in turn has a return effect from mental to physical. This is the cycle that you start to go through. I believe it is important for family members to say if they see any changes, although this can be very hard to talk about. It is important to talk and to do this in a suitable manner. I asked Debra, my wife, if she saw any changes in my persona and she replied that I was going at things 'like a bull in a china shop'. However, I may have been like that for some years. This can build up over years. I would think it would be very hard to see, but we need people to understand that what goes on in the mind can be so destructive, but because you cannot see it like a broken leg, does not make it non-existent. Let us end this notion that we are crazy.

One of the last comments in the book is from when Dad was in hospital:

> 'Dad phoned after lunch saying a Dr. was very nasty towards him and told him to go back to bed or sign himself out'.

From the dates in the book, it is clear that this happened on the 27th October 1995. My dad passed away a few weeks later on the 19th December 1995. In my opinion no matter how ill people feel no matter from what they are suffering, they deserve respect which should be given. However I appreciate that there are two opinions to every story.

After Dad passed away, Mum moved out of the family home, where I grew up, into sheltered accommodation. Our family home was the end house and unfortunately although Mum had some great neighbours in the past, many had now moved. There were only a few left, and the ones that Mum new quite well lived at the end of the street, which was split, by another road. This was quite a distance away and Mum only saw these people now and again. I believe she felt isolated there so Mum moved into the sheltered accommodation and settled in very well and very quickly.

The accommodation was monitored twenty-four hours a day. The manager was a lovely woman and there were people in there that Mum knew from her past. In fact this place was not far from the first home that Mum and Dad moved into after living with my dad's parents for some time. Mum had the opportunity to be on her own or if she wished there were regular activities which took place.

It was not until Mum moved there, that I actually sat down and really chatted with her. I found this very interesting and informative. It is perhaps that in the past we were just too concerned with our own lives, which I believe happens to many people as we grow old too quickly. The last place she lived consisted of a joint bedroom and lounge, together with a bathroom, toilet and kitchen. I believe she was quite happy there and met some fine people. Mum missed Dad terribly. I can still see her sitting in the chair in the room, with the sunshine coming through the window. We visited as often as we could. My oldest sister would always try and pop in after work. I know that Dad was never far from her mind, like the rest of the family. Was Mum suffering 'the agony within'? I just do not know.

There came a point, when Mum seemed to be in and out of hospital, all the time. She would improve and she would come out, but it would not be long before she was re-admitted. I remember the end quite vividly. Mum had decided that she would not take any further medication. Her arms where quite badly bruised. This must have been the second time she had been admitted to hospital in quick succession. I asked her why she would not take her medication and she simply said that she had reached a point, where it was too much for her. I did not realize at the time what this really meant. I soon found out. Mum became worse and fell asleep on the 2nd January 2000. I found this very hard to accept. This episode played on my mind for quite some time. With Dad I think we were just expecting it. I loved my mum immensely.

I think no matter what age you are to lose a parent is quite devastating, I suppose it depends on your relationship with them, but I am certain it can contribute to 'the agony within'.

The Agony Within

Chapter Eight: Death

I think that the first time that death affected me was my grandfather's death, on my dad's side of the family. He had been quite ill for some time and I would go with Dad to visit him in hospital. I was a young boy of about fifteen years old. The hospital was a dull and depressing place. I sat next to my granddad's side in the hospital and some words that struck me were when he said that he could see the angels were coming for him and it was his time to go. At this point, as a young lad, you can understand that my first thoughts were that Granddad was going a bit mad. As we were about to leave and Granddad had settled down, I spoke to Dad about what granddad had said. We put it down to the reflection in the ceiling from the lights. I think that death plays a part in 'the agony within'.

I think it was the next day, that we had the news that granddad had died during the night. It was quite odd, the way that I felt, yes I shed a few tears. I sat on the stairs, as this was a place that I found myself at times, just thinking about many issues, probably worrying about things that may not happen. As I am writing this I can feel my heart pumping and I am not sure why. Well that was it. Granddad is dead, so is that what life is all about? You just end up dead? This thought began to make me feel sick and I could not get it out of my head. My thoughts were that you were born, you grow old and die. At this point I could feel myself beginning to panic somewhat and I could not control it. Just writing about it now, makes me feel really odd. I do not think that I have ever lost that feeling. There I was sat on the stairs and did not know, what I wanted to do. These thoughts are still going through my head, why will it not stop? Please make it stop! Please someone help me with the way that I feel. This is the first time that I have put this to paper and to be honest I find that I cannot type the words fast enough.

You may ask yourself why I did not say anything to Mum and Dad. I do not know. Was it that I thought that I would make myself look a fool? Was I just growing up? Perhaps if I had said something then would I have felt better? This is something that I will never know. At this point, writing this, I feel so angry. It makes me think if I had said something, then things would be different. Was this the start of 'the agony within'? Yes I used to keep a lot of things under my hat. As I became older this feeling about Granddad and death stayed with me for some time.

Chapter Nine: Working too hard

So, I had been on nights at *Butts* regularly for nine years and it suited me, Debra, and the two daughters we now had; Rosie and Roberta. Then suddenly the management structure changed and I believe that many employees believed that the company wanted to eject the high earners. It is questionable whether they would get caught; we had a union but it was a waste of time, as several employees felt they the union were in the management's pockets, particularly when the union representative's son acquired an excellent job. We were told that there would be changes whether we liked it or not. There was some pontificating by some employees but it was all bluff. As the old saying goes, 'someone would load the gun, but then let someone else shoot the bullets'.

At first the night shift was informed that things would change, from four nights to five, as the management wanted Friday night covered. Honestly we could not see the point and we even informed the management of our reasons which included facts and figures. We became suspicious of Derek, the nightshift supervisor, as he did not disagree and even thought it was a good idea. As I mentioned, he had his own agenda. The changes disrupted our weekends, as I did not arrive home until 4am. During this time nothing happened to the two day shifts I wonder why? Was it because of the union man? That shift did not last long and once again the night shift was informed that the shift was to change. Again there a pattern; the shift was 6pm till 2am, because of the distance that I had to cover and how busy the motorway was, it could take me three hours to get there but we agreed; we did not have a choice. After a while, something strange happened. A few of the workers on the other two shifts had their shifts altered, and it meant that some of them would lose quite a lot of their wages through shift allowance. The workers were not keen on this and it must have been hard for them, because they could lose up to a hundred pounds per week. It is perhaps that the management offered these lads an exit route. The business was not that good and I think that we all could see what was to happen. Those workers, whose shifts had suddenly changed, were being offered redundancy and because some of them had been there some years, they would get a large amount, but that does not help if you are losing your job. It is alleged that those lads received an extra payment, if they signed an agreement to say that they would take voluntary redundancy, so in fact the company had removed some of the high earners.

Eventually the workers on nights including myself were told that we were going to be amalgamated with the two day shifts. This was not unexpected, but in the meantime the company had employed short term workers who were eventually made permanent, but on lower wages than us and who we were informed that we had to train. The things that were going through my mind, such as: How long do I have left? Will they need me? It was clear the fear of losing my job had put me on high alert. Arthur and I were split up, with him and Derek on one shift and me on another. Although I knew my co-workers, it was like starting a job all over again, for I had to prove myself to a new supervisor. He, Stuart, was a nice chap, but was a workaholic. He gave the impression that he never had time for anyone. However, Malcolm whom I now worked with, I could relate to, as he was always trying hard and like myself, wanted to keep his job. When I started with Stuart it was as if I was just dumped in there and I think this was the start of my breakdown. No matter what I did it just did not seem to be recognised but despite this the new management did send me on a team building course. I think that I just showed that I could be worth more than what I was doing. I did a few presentations with the workers on the shop floor, but some did not like the idea, because I believed I was some sort of spy for the workforce, well that is how I felt.

All I ever wanted was to do a good job, to the best of my ability. With this is the feeling of being needed and wanted, but I felt I was not getting this and no matter what I did at work, it was not being noted. It felt that most of the lads were just fighting to keep their jobs and would do anything to stay and if you were unlucky to be in the way they would trample over you. I think I was missing my best mate Arthur, as he was on the other shift. Perhaps he had the better shift than me, as he could talk to Derek. However, I actually felt a bit sorry for him, as he had tried his hardest to get into a senior role, but this never materialised. Perhaps they should have put him in charge; he would have been fair but firm. I think that some people who had a job there after the redundancies were either liars or told the management what they wanted to hear. From the side lines this only added pressure on me to perform and ensure work was right, but there was never anyone to say the work produced was acceptable and at this point I needed that. It reached a point where if they had said my work was to a good standard, then I would not have believed them. I needed trust and I am afraid I did not feel I was receiving it.

Each day the trip to work became harder and harder. The motorway seemed busier as days passed and it often felt like I had done a shift before I reached work. I would find myself yawning and not being able to catch my breath. I did visit the doctors and he gave me an inhaler, similar to those which asthma sufferers carry, but I do not think it worked. This is the start of a period of time where I cannot remember much.

One thing that disgusted me was during the drive to work, on the motorway, the traffic would always be at a standstill in the same place. This had happened before, like the time I was coming home just before my second daughter Roberta was born and I was stuck on the motorway for about three and a half hours. A lorry driver kindly allowed me use of his cab telephone, to contact Debra to make sure she was not worried.

On the way to work on a different occasion, the weather was not that good and all I can remember was how I had to get to work and what would happen if I was late. The management would reprimand you and workers would have to complete overtime for the lost time, although this did not apply to everyone. This was just one of the many aspects that used to irritate myself and Arthur so during my motorway journeys, all that I could think about was work. We were still edging up the motorway and at last we moved along a bit quicker, then I began to see why, there had been some road works. However, that was an understatement; the motorway seemed to be a practice area for work men. There was a large blue sheet covering over one of the cars. I thought they covered the cars when there was a death. There must have been seven or eight cars involved. I could see suitcases sprawled all over the place. As I passed by I felt great sadness, who would not? The disgust I felt with myself for feeling selfish when I realised that all I was interested in was arriving at work. My thoughts had been that I had to reach there, as quickly as possible. In my life I had seen many road accidents, but this time just seemed to hit me harder.

I remember the occasion very well and now I think it still slightly affects me. That night I could not get the image out of my head and how all I had wanted to do was get to work, which was the most important thing, I am sorry to admit this, but yes as stupid as it seems. It is clear that the obsession of work stood in the way of actually enjoying life at home. It was as if I was thinking about work day and night. It is quite odd, but it actually became a drug; my head was just full of worry about work. My life would operate like this: get up in the morning and think what you might encounter at work. Should I ring them? Will I get up the motorway? Did I make any errors the night before? What has been said? Can I keep my job? Do we have plenty of work? Am I producing enough? Is it good enough for the management? What do they think of me? When I first wrote this part, I did not put any punctuation in there. This is what my brain was like; it would not stop to rest. It was hard to think, but it felt like my brain was full all the time. I was constantly thinking and worrying and if I had nothing to worry about, then I was worried because of that. It became clear that this had been building up for some time.

The Agony Within

Chapter Ten: Feeling unwell

I remember one point at work where I was literally running about. It is still a bit vague, but that is etched in my memory. It was April 2003 and I was still employed at *Butts*. I woke up at my normal time on the Monday, for I was on the afternoon shift that week. I had to ring my wife Debra to tell her that I felt unwell and I was having breathing problems and had chest pains. It was very scary. On Debra's request I visited my doctor, with whom I had a good relationship and he signed me off sick for a week. Now, regarding this period of my life, I cannot tell you everything that happened. It is not that I do not want too; it is just a bit vague. I remember talking to my doctor at one point and I just broke down. On that day I telephoned work to explain that I would not be in for some time and broke down again. I am not sure why, it was just one of those occurrences that you cannot explain. Initially the doctor signed me off for a week, which became a fortnight, then three months and eventually I was on long-term sick.

When I was originally signed off sick, I had medical insurance, so we took the option to have my heart and breathing checked which seemed to take weeks. I was booked into a private hospital in Leicester (although after a year, when my cover ceased and I was back to the NHS, interesting that I felt the care was just as good). Yes I was lucky and I mean very lucky that for long term sickness, my employer *Butts* had the insurance cover which would pay half of my wages. It was a struggle but receiving half was better than nothing. This is perhaps now easy for me to say, but circumstances were very tight at the time.

During the time that I was off work, the management at *Butts* treated me well. However I had to visit the doctor every three months and I believed that this was to prove to the insurance company that I was ill. I know this did not help. Why did I have to prove anything? I believe it took all of my energy to understand or try to understand what was going wrong with my life. In my head this was just an additional aspect to add to 'the agony within'.

Looking back it does seem that I spent the whole of the first year, having tests. For instance, during the time at the private hospital in Leicester, I was booked in for an angiogram, which is where a small wire is fed in at the groin and up to the heart. This is all done whilst you are awake and it is visible on a screen. During the operation the doctor informed me that other than one slightly furred artery, that everything was in normal order. Once again I felt disappointed. I was still looking for something physically wrong with me. After leaving the doctor a nurse put her fist in my groin for fifteen minutes, so the artery could heal. Then I had to lie on my back for three hours, during which Debra sat with me. Looking back she must have been going through hell.

At the end of the three hours, which was actually closer to three and a half, Debra and I were both starving. The nurses allowed me to sit up, at last. We both had a cup of tea and a different packet of sandwiches. I was just about to swap with Debra when she asked how I felt. I told her that I did feel a bit odd and for some reason Debra lifted the sheet only to find that my artery had burst. She yelled out for help, as I began to feel myself drifting away. When I woke I found one nurse was inserting a drip and the other was sitting on top of me, with her fist in my groin. I reassured Debra that if this was the way you pass away, then you would not know anything about it. The nurses asked how I felt, which was not good, so they decided it was in my best interest to stay in for the night which meant Debra had to drive home on unfamiliar roads. Debra reassured me that she would be able to make the journey; I had all my faith in her that she could do it, but I still worried about her. I do not believe my daughters really knew what was going on and I think that was a bad idea. All I wanted to do was to protect my girls. I thought that to tell them about it was too frightening or was I dwelling in the thought that I could have died. How do you tell two young girls that you thought you were going to die? I did not want to put that thought into their heads, but looking back perhaps I should have told them. I am still here to tell the story. I was doing something that we automatically do and that is to protect children from the word *death*. Now I think this is wrong; it is acceptable, if it is put over in the right way.

Where my daughters are concerned, I have held back about some of my dark periods. I think that the burst artery was out of my hands, and you could say that my dark periods were, but the burst artery to a degree, could be described as exciting, scary or funny. Luckily, it was something to talk about that took my mind away from the way that I was feeling.

There must have been something in my brain that wanted to protect the girls. I did not want to involve them; perhaps there was a safety switch. It was during my dark periods that the thought of my girls came into my brain and it sort of protected me, which is the only thing that I can think of. At times it must have been upsetting for my wife, but I always felt that she was the strong one, she is to a degree. I feel that I owe her so much; well she saved my life.

The night passed without incidence and Debra reached home safely. The next day, we were both given instructions, mine was the usual hospital to patient instructions, but Debra had specific instructions, which included special pads and what to do if my artery burst during the drive home. Debra would have to stop the car on the motorway hard shoulder, put me on my back on the floor and use the pads and a fist to thrust into my groin. Debra later admitted that it was one of the worst journeys that she had ever experienced. Each time I had moved or twitched she was nervous.

Following this I actually tried to go back to work at *Butts* a few times without success. I had panic attacks, breathing problems and was unable to drive on the motorway, which for some reason scared the life out of me. As you might understand I could not make sense of it and this was one of the reasons that I could not return to work. It is quite funny, as I write this; I can remember it quite well. It is like a mist, when you are trying so hard to return to work, but there is this invisible wall that is stopping you. I may have glossed over the months that I was off and visiting the hospital, but it just went so quickly. I was actually hoping they would find something wrong with me and it would explain why I felt, the way that I did.

The doctor always referred to my illness as anxiety and depression. I feel that he never really spoke about it too much. He was just mainly concerned that he was improving my health. I think that you will agree that even using the words anxiety and depression is bad enough; well this was what was put on my sick notes. As you have read, it took some time to find out that it was. Not my heart or lungs; it was my mind.

To hear the doctor say you have a broken leg, does not sound that bad, as you know it will fix in time; but as we know there is no time limit on anxiety and depression (or a breakdown), and this can scare even more. It may well do without realizing, because to be fair I do not think anyone truly knows why this happens, because to this day I cannot definitely say what started 'the agony within'.

The Agony Within

Chapter Eleven: Belief

I think that I have always believed in Jesus; my wife is catholic and so are my two children. This does not bother me at all because if I had been born into any other religion, I think that I would have believed in that. Living next door to a church did not encourage me to visit the church, but I always admired our local priest. He is a very kind man who put a great deal into the local community. I remember when my father was ill; he found solace in the church. One day I had visited my parents and Mum informed me that Dad had gone to church. He was not well and I believe he thought that a visit to church would help him. Mum always said that when he had been to church, he returned more content and felt better; a lot of the pain had gone. Was this Jesus doing his job? I would like to think so.

In the early stages of my illness I just could not understand what was happening to me. To say I was confused would be an understatement. My doctor had recommended that I should go and seek help in the form of a counsellor, which actually horrified me. The suggestion that I should visit a counsellor made me wonder if the doctor was suggesting that I was going mad. I mulled this over for some months and at this point decided to go to the church that was next door to my old family home. I just felt that I needed some help and thought that it might assist in the form of prayer. I walked in and sat down and luckily I was the only one there. I felt myself well up and I started to cry. I asked if there was some way that God could help me, with the way that I felt, which included my guilt. I felt I had disappointed my wife and children, plus I felt that it was my fault that my mum had passed away. Then I became aware of Reverend Sneath, he was our local

Church of England vicar and a good friend to all on the estate where we had lived; he had also performed the funeral service for both my mum and dad. The Reverend asked me how I was feeling, and then if I would I like to talk, which I did. He also asked me if he could lay his hands on my head and say a prayer, to which I agreed. Why did I agree? That is something that I perhaps will never understand.

I have mentioned that I had experienced some 'dark thoughts'; I call them that because I did not understand why I would want to take my own life, and believe me if you have had those thoughts, you would understand what I am talking about. The best way that I can try to explain, is that it was when I wanted to do harm to myself. There just seemed to be a very quick rush of thought that went through my mind without warning. It only took place a couple of times, but was enough to frighten me. Even typing this and trying to explain, I find quite difficult. I have tried to include further details for you, and admit that at first I was reluctant to do so. However I feel it is important to try and explain in the event that you ever experience these feelings. Perhaps not everyone has these thoughts, but if you do you must talk about them. I believe these thoughts can be self-destructive and to this day I still cannot understand why they happened. Perhaps I was lucky, in that I am still here, however I do not truly believe it was luck; it is just a thought. What I do know is that at the time my thoughts reverted to my family. It was the love of my wife and two daughters that kept me going. Without, what I call my 'three girls', things may have been a bit different.

After leaving the church I felt somewhat calmer, this was when I decided to visit the local town and book myself into the counsellor's; it was based at a charity, to which I was originally referred by my Doctor. It was really quite strange; I still could not understand why I should go. There I was in the town and heading for the centre; I stood by the door for some fifteen minutes before I rang the bell. After I rang the bell, I awaited someone to see me, only to be told that the centre was in the process of moving and I had to go to a different place further down the road. I dreaded the thought that I had to go through all of that again, but I had to try to do this. This time it was straight to the door, I think that it was open as there was building work taking place. This was the first time I met Jill my counsellor; she made it so easy. I was falling apart whilst Jill ushered me into a room, where I broke down and was blabbering in a very quick manner. I did not realise that Jill was assessing both me and the situation but at the end of it, Jill informed me, that she was happy to take me on as a client although I doubt that Jill would put it that way. When I walked out of there, I felt both relief and confusion. What was I letting myself in for? More than that, was Jill going to be able to sort me out in a couple of weeks?

At the time I was looking for Jill to solve all my problems. When I say problems, I mean sort my head out. How wrong I was! At first it seemed as if I just could not stop talking, about everything including my wife Debra and my two daughters, work and the death of my parents. However work was the major thing. My head at times was so full of thoughts that I wondered if it might burst. One aspect that did worry me was what affect this was all this having on family. I tried to be as honest as I could, with the girls, because I did not want to frighten them. However, at the beginning I kept a few things back from Debra, because they were not nice thoughts, including those about taking my own life. Now as I type this, that thought makes me shudder, but I can understand it more. I always related to that type of thinking as my 'dark thoughts'.

The Agony Within

Chapter Twelve: Luck

I was very lucky that I had two school friends that I had known since the age of four. One was Gordon and the other was Ken. They were different, but the same in that with them I was able to talk. Despite Gordon's battle with cancer he made time for me. I think that we did each other some good, just sitting in the sunshine drinking tea and having a laugh. Actually I could write a book about Gordon and myself. Some people wondered how he coped with his cancer, but he was a fighter and he would not let anything beat him; he was very competitive. He lost his battle in 2005 and this was during the time that I was off work and it hindered my recovery. I was very close to him and loved him, in the right way. Ken I knew, like Gordon, but we actually lost touch, until we met at a school reunion in the year 2000 and decided that we would rekindle our friendship. He is also one of those that you can say anything to and that is as far as it goes. With both Gordon and Ken, they never made me feel stupid, a bit daft maybe, but I think you need someone to talk to, not to try and understand, just to talk.

I probably know that I did not talk that much to my wife, not that I did not want to. I think that I was trying to protect her and not let her worry but she could read me like a book; she told me that as soon as I woke up, she knew what sort of day I would have. When you are in that position, you are unclear what to do for the best. I think you just shut up and be quiet, believing that the situation would get better. I would not try to tell anyone what to do, yes go and get some specific support, but that would be all my advice. I think it would be too easy to influence people. One of the main aspects that I have found with Jill is that she never once told me what I should do. As the months went on, I began to realise that it was me that had to work things out.

I realise that visiting Jill was one of the most important things that I could have done. Without her help and care I do not think that I would be where I am today. Jill was a true professional. I admit that I cannot remember all that I said during the countless sessions. I am sure that I may have repeated myself at times. I do believe that the one-to-one sessions are a very private and personal thing, and to try and write what happened during these discussions would not sit comfortably with me. It is possible that for Jill some of the symptoms she witnesses may be the same, but the person sitting opposite is a different one, and the counsellor would have to react to different situations and thus the conversations would be very individual. However, one of the sayings that has remained with me, that Jill used was 'at this moment in time'. This is so true on reflection and I will explain. I believe that you cannot help what has happened and you do not know about tomorrow, so it is about how you feel at that moment in time. To focus on that, is the best thing that you can do.

I had an occasion where I had to visit a different counsellor, for reasons unknown to me and I was not sure why I was recommended to her. A time might arise where you are not happy with your counsellor and then you must admit this. The lady was of foreign nationality and I felt so uncomfortable with this, perhaps as I believed that I had to explain myself, which I felt hindered my progress. I went back to Jill, or I felt that I needed to go back to Jill. I feel this relationship is important and so if you are not happy, you must try to speak out. However, overall I do believe though that if individuals are recommended to go to a counsellor, then they should try to do this.

For me I think that through my life I have always been told what to do and to a degree that worked until I had my breakdown. It was the oddest feeling that you could have. Although Jill never did this, there was one aspect that Jill pointed me towards, which was the local college, although this was quite a frightening thing, as I was still having problems in meeting people. I could not even visit the local store, to purchase groceries. This would never happen. I would visit with Debra and it was so queer, I could not get my breath properly and things would start to spin around. I could not wait to get out. How she coped with this, I will never ever know. I remember I visited the college and asked about the courses; my heart pounded and my eyes were all over the place. What was wrong? Come on! I thought; you can do this. I acquired the information and explained that if I may appear a bit odd, it was due to my condition. The lady receptionist put me at my ease, gave me the details I needed. I walked out as quickly as possible, as I could not wait for the fresh air.

At one point I was referred to a psychiatrist, it was probably during the second year, and I only visited about five times. However for me I felt that I had to repeat what I had said to my doctor and counsellor. All I seemed to have received was medication. I am not sure what I thought I would get out of the psychiatrist, help and a cure perhaps.

I had tried other agencies for help, but I felt the service they believed I required was not the sort of help that I needed. Do not misunderstand me; I thought they acted very professionally. I visited a place in the adjoining town, to where I live and I felt very nervous about it. I went past the place several times before I went in. When I did, it was like I had hit a brick wall; the place was packed with people with all sorts of problems, some worse than me and others who were not as bad, but who am I to say who was ill and who was not? This place catered for all, from diabetes to learning difficulties and I wondered where I figured in this. I felt the people who ran the centre had a difficult task on their hands. There was one particular young lady who I would say had learning difficulties. She tried and succeeded in making me feel welcome and had a charm about her that seemed to shine. I still felt anxious; it was as if my whole body could not keep still. My brain was full of what would happen: Who it will be? Was I in the correct place? Should I be here? What will happen? Then again my brain was full like that, most of the time.

All of a sudden a face caught my eye, which seemed familiar. She came over to me and I said hello and gave her a kiss; we knew each other some twenty-five years ago. It was Jackie, who used to be my brother-in-law's girlfriend and although I had not seen her for some time, it was nice to see someone that I knew. She ushered me into an office for a chat. She was not the one I was due to see. I explained why I was there and told her about my breakdown. She was very sympathetic and went to find out when the person that I was meeting would be there. It only seemed like five minutes before he turned up and Jackie introduced me to him. He was a young man, in his twenties and very well turned out, but the odd thing was he seemed as nervous as me. We went to another office and had a chat, and then arranged another meeting, which was in front of a different young lady. What I found with this was that I seemed to be explaining all the time, why I was there. I had several meetings with them, but soon realised that the help that they wanted to give me was not the help I required. They would help me to write a reference and look for jobs, but I felt that at that time, it was not for me. I was in a very odd situation as my previous employer was still paying me through an insurance company, which was half of my wages. This I was very grateful for, but the company would make me redundant as soon as I classed myself fit for work. It was a catch; get well and lose your job. Jill my counsellor had recognised this fact, and to be fair, what could she do? We could not arrange a phased return to work. This is one of the reasons that I believe why I was off sick, for so long. So we recognised that it was up to me to get myself back to work.

All I wanted to do was go to bed, as early as I could, sometimes as early as 8 pm. I would stay in bed for as long as possible; I felt safe there. The nights were drawing in and I felt safe in the dark. Leaving the house was a challenge. I would have been quite happy not to go anywhere. In addition, was the fact that a visit to the shop was very difficult, as I did not want to drive. As time progressed, I was happy enough around the town, but the thought of using the motorway, really scared me. This did not help with regard to my job at *Butts*, as it was an eighty mile round trip. My doctor recommended that I should visit a group called *Astra*, which I did, but it was another one of those where you had to go and meet people. I really did not know what to expect, but there were people there with similar feelings to me. What it did was let me know that I was not the only person, who felt the way that I did. We were taught certain exercises to do and breathing was a prominent theme. There was also a chap there that like me could not face the drive on the motorway. I must admit that I cannot tell you much about what happened, because as I write this, I can only remember parts of it.

I told Jill about *Astra* and how I was not sure if it was for me. At no time did Debra or my daughters, question me about the chats with Jill. I would only say that it went well, but it must have been odd for Debra because there was me visiting Jill to divulge everything. Debra was one hell of a rock. I found that my eldest sister would ask me questions that I could not answer. Debra even told my sister that if I did not have the answer for her, who would, I have it for? There was one phrase that I learned and I still use it today. For some people it might seem daft, but for me it was both important and true and it was that which Jill used ("at this moment in time"). I feel that is quite a valuable phrase and I will explain, I had difficulty in explaining, where I was and who I was. This may seem a bit odd, but that is how I felt at the time. Everything that my mind was going through was just unbelievable. I must admit, I cannot remember everything.

This episode had given me the chance to meet some people who I would never have met. You do not realize how many people out there are involved in jobs which aim to help others. It also gave me a chance to sit down and have a heart to heart chat with some great people in my life. I think there is always a certain amount of luck found in having such good friends and family. However sometimes you make your own luck in life. If this episode had not happened when it did, but when I was younger I could not have coped with it. I was very lucky to have Debra by my side.

Chapter Thirteen: Getting better

At times I felt better, but there are still highs and lows. To a certain extent, I was frightened to get better, because the thought of falling back to where I was, filled me so full of dread.

The adulation that you feel, when you have a good day is quite unbelievable. There is this rush, where you just want to do everything. The feeling is that good, but it can be spoilt by one simple thought and if it is a doubting thought, then there is only one way, that you can go and that is downhill fast. Trying to cope with this and live day to day puts a strain on you and your family. You cannot explain why this happens and even to this day, I still cannot tell you.

The exact date of this I cannot recall, but I think it was towards the time when I was feeling better and I could feel that I was. However, it may have been with Jill or one of the other agencies that I visited, but we were chatting about how I felt at that moment in time and the words depression and anxiety came into play and Jill said that in her opinion I had suffered a breakdown. I am not sure if at one of my meetings with the psychiatrist that the word breakdown had also been used. However I do not feel these words were used lightly. Perhaps individuals have to be careful on what words they use to explain about how you feel at that moment in time, because 'the agony within' is real.

I remember going for a walk, which I was told, by my counsellor or one of the groups I visited, that it was one of the best things for you. That is acceptable if the illness allows you to go outside of your home. One time I noticed the strangest things; the sky looked blue, I mean really blue and the clouds looked lovely, just like when I used to lie on the back lawn at my parents' house. I think that you have to want to get better, which may sound a bit odd, but I seemed to have been in the darkness for some time. Then there was this blast of colour. To say it was fantastic to see that blue sky would be an understatement. I suddenly realised that the world looked good. I cannot tell you why this happened. At that point I had to ask myself if it was real, as I did not want the feeling to end.

Since January 2007, I have had that feeling of getting better, then it was the November, so if you think that it happens over night, then it did not happen like that for me.

Chapter Fourteen: Getting back to work

As I started to feel better during early 2007, I knew that I wanted to return to work. To do this I realized that I would have to arrange a meeting with my line manager at *Butts* which I did. I drove myself to work for the meeting; it was about a forty mile journey there or eighty on a round trip, but I drove myself this distance, as I felt much better. However, there was so much going through my mind that I cannot remember much about the journey itself. I was nervous but I managed to keep myself calm and my breathing as gentle as I could. I stepped out of the car, took some deep breaths and made my way to the reception. It felt odd. I walked to the reception desk and was greeted by an unfamiliar face. It was clear that some changes had taken place, since I was last there. In the four years that I was off, I had only been to work a few times, when I had attempted to return there previously; the majority of conversations were held over the telephone.

I was shown to my line manager's office where I was greeted in a pleasant manner. He was the perfect gent. I was offered and accepted a drink and I sat down. He asked me how I felt and I told him that I was a bit nervous, but felt good. One of the main aspects on my mind was the desire to return to work, not that I needed to, but that I wanted to. For me it was important to be financially secure and back to normal, whatever that might have been. However I knew that work was not the number one thing in my life; it was my wife and family. My line manager and I started to make small talk and even today I find it easy to talk about my illness; for I believe that it is something that is often pushed aside. As the conservation developed he informed me that his wife had been poorly. Was this just small talk or did he need to tell me? Then we moved onto the serious part of the visit: getting back to work.

I was torn. I wanted to return and I knew the job well. However I did not want the eighty mile round trip. There would be triggers in there which would send me back to the place that I had been for the last four years. Did the company want me back? Would they see me as a risk? I think that 'the agony within' has such a stigma attached to it, which fuelled these questions in me. He asked me directly if I wanted to return to my old job. I could not give him a definite yes.

I had started the road to recovery. I was able to make a proper decision without jumping in. I had started to look after myself. That is a key aspect, not to just try to please others and say what you may think what they want to hear, but to look after yourself. I was still employed, but I knew that I could not go back there; life was so up and down. Since my illness began in April 2003, I was lucky that the firm had kept me employed, during the time that I was off. The half pay I received had really helped. It was quite odd in a way; sometimes I wanted to return to work, then I would just slip back into something that I could not handle. I was continually divided. Deep down they had already made their decision and did not want me back, and I do not believe that I wanted the job.

However I was taken aback by a comment from my line manager when he asked if he had contributed to my illness, with everything that had happened there. I paused to think about this, but informed him that I could not honestly say. I think that this had been with me for quite some time. Was it the trigger? Today as I write this then it could have been, but in all honesty I was unable to place the weight of blame for what happened on him. It would have been easy, to blame him or the company, but I have been asked many times and still to this day I honestly cannot be sure. I told my line manager that I believed it was not just one issue but a build up of numerous issues that happened through my life, which decided to take effect on me, in my forties. With this type of illness there is no time scale and it gives you no warning; it just smacks you down with a sledge hammer.

The meeting ended well and it was decided that I should come over and see him again. I cannot remember if we decided that I was not going to return at that meeting or at the next one but I did leave. I do not hold any grudges. Why should I? Life is for living. After driving back from that first meeting I knew and felt that I was well on my way back to being or feeling better. It was good, I had my life back. It is still quite odd, that now I do feel different about life in general. I enjoy and love life.

Despite my inability to determine the trigger for what happened, the thought that my company wanted to get rid of me, did play quite a major role in my thoughts. If like me, work has played a major role in your life, then you may have lost the feeling of being needed or wanted. Yes, the term *wanted*, may seem a bit strong, but for a man of my generation, that is very important. For some months, I have been in hyper drive. I told my family that I needed to go back to work. Easy some might say...

The Agony Within

Chapter Fifteen: Being judged

Being judged is possibly a personal thing, but I have always felt whatever I have done someone was there looking over my shoulder. For instance, interviews; now there is something that I have learned. I was so nervous at one where I had to do a simple test. I had to use both hands to steady the pen, so I could complete the test. I felt so stupid. This interview was in two parts, the first was a written test and then an interview, on a one-to-one basis. I passed the first part and achieved thirty-eight out of forty. It was easy, so maybe I should have achieved forty. My two daughters could have done it, with their eyes closed. I went onto the next part; I was so nervous and thought that things were going well, until they questioned me about the time absent from work, during the last twelve months. I informed them that I had been off for the past year due to a breakdown of anxiety and depression or whatever you call it. Then I saw it in their eyes. It was clear their response would mean that I would go to the bottom of the list. It was apparent without them uttering a word.

Odd people that I have spoken to, but not all, when they hear the words breakdown, their eyes will show what they really think. Yes I was told that I had all the qualifications that I needed to do the job, but then I was turned down. People in my position have been short changed by this government. When watching the television, the Prime Minister said that the government was working with major supermarkets and other stores to create jobs. Personally, I have no objection to working in a store, I have done it for a number of years, but the pay and hours are inadequate. Where are all the manufacturing jobs? However, I will not speak any more about MPs government or anything like it, because those people do not appear in tune with reality. As long as they receive their huge salaries, they do not care. It seems at present, that the only way a fifty-one year old male can acquire a job, is be a parcel handler for an agency or to go into security.

Chapter Sixteen: It never goes away

I have been doing my current job, as a school caretaker, since December 2007 and I have not had a day off sick. But last week after feeling unwell for some two weeks and after visiting the doctors, I had a muscle spasm, which really hurt. I was lucky because the other caretaker at work was just at the end of the telephone and he came in to work, as soon as he could. It hurt me to think that I had to take time off. I visited the doctor and told him how I felt, because of the time that I had off work. I suppose it frightened me. I feel that he gave me some tablets that fixed me pretty quick and I wonder if he gave them to me, because he could see how taking time off work, was affecting me. My boss was very understanding and wished me well. Although I only had two days off, I feel it has affected me.

With my family, we sat down and watched an episode of a television programme entitled *The Secret Millionaire*. There was a dad who was an alcoholic and he said how it affected his life and his family's lives and how his own dad had killed himself. The programme affected me and the next day before I went to work I had a couple of panic attacks and yes it was scary. I understood what was happening, which does not make you feel any better, but my wife and daughter were there. I told them how I was feeling. My daughter was watching a rerun of *The Secret Millionaire* episode that we had watched last night. I said that there was not much difference between an alcoholic and a workaholic; the effects are the same and they are both very destructive. When you have the condition, you cannot be without that which feeds it, work or alcohol. With this person losing their father to alcoholism, and with my experience, I know how close you can come to it. I still do not understand why; I think that it just hit me that this person died and his family were left to grieve. I think when I talk about the dark periods, that programme brought it home to me. I think this is the first time that I have called myself a workaholic and I have admitted to Debra that this does not go away. The way that I feel at the moment is quite odd, I feel as if I am starting my job all over again.

There are occasions when I feel very angry, at the way that I felt at a particular time. As I write this I can feel myself trying, but not really understanding why. Is this normal? Well why not? You are having your life turned upside down. Well it felt like that.

So it never goes away because, it is something that you will always carry with you and it just depends on how you feel with regard to talking about it. In my experience it does get better. I think sometimes I am quite proud to talk about it, to a degree. I have come through possibly one of the worst times in my life. This may sound a bit dramatic, but it was, at the time to me. I still have to stand back and take a few deep breaths. To this day, when I talk about this period I start to yawn. I am not sure why.

Chapter Seventeen: Dark thoughts and death

I think looking back when I was poorly, sometimes death was the easy option. They were my dark times and it is really odd when it hits you out of the blue. I think that we are expected that we should accept that we are born and then we die. Yes we know that as a fact, but we are never taught how to handle it, especially when your mum or dad dies. Yes, we all accept that we take it for granted, that parents are expected to die before their children. Yes in some or a lot of cases this does not happen. How are you supposed to handle the fact that someone you love dearly is not there anymore? The fact that we know that it is going to happen, does not help. I feel that we are not told some of the feelings that we may have; it affects us all in different ways. Some people perhaps do not like to talk about it, in fear that it will happen. The guilt of not saying how much you love them or even just talking to them, perhaps we have lost the ability to chat to one another in our busy lives or are too busy to even chat. I must admit that I tell my wife and daughters how much I love them, as often as I can but even in the job that I am in, it sometimes gets in the way and you have to take a step back.

Last year, I learned that a young girl at school died from cancer. We may have spoken, I am not sure. In a 1200 pupil school, you just never know. Some stand out more than others. It does make you think how lucky we are. My heart goes out to the young girl's family and I cannot begin to think how they must be feeling. On my wife's side, her cousin lost her teenage son in action, whilst serving in the army. Looking back, this makes me feel a bit selfish in wanting to do something to myself, but in hindsight that is easy to say. But what I feel now is that I love life more than anything else. An old saying is that *life is for living* and I think sometimes, we have lost the ability to do this, because we are so wrapped up with work, maintaining and paying for a home and all the rest that we believe we go to work for. Just looking at the television whilst writing this, sometimes I think that it is the worst thing that you could have in the house. Yes it can bring some enjoyment and laughter, but it is the easy way out. We really depend on it to give us so much information and sometimes I feel it provides a falsehood about life and death. How many times have we been told, on the news that someone has died and we just pass it over, as if it has happened to someone else? But that is just it, we are not prepared when it happens to us, it really hits you hard.

It is perhaps that society gives us the impression that we should just accept matters, when a death occurs. However I believe that the subject of death is taboo in a lot of households, who may fear that something awful will happen. Why can we not be told the truth that death strikes at any time? We may not like it, but it is not about trying to scare anyone. To a certain degree children are protected from the word. I am not saying that we should banter it about. You may ask at what age we should learn about death. Perhaps it should be taught at junior school, between the ages of seven and eleven. I know that children see it on the television but to be fair it never looks real. Even on some of the old fashioned games, computer games that children play or in movies, they show death in a light way, as people then come back to life. When I was a child we would play war games or cowboys and Indians, yes we were possibly no different than now. Where we should be different is not hiding the fact about death, for it does not assist 'the agony within'.

Chapter Eighteen: Here and now

Now I feel I have had chance to actually relax and I do not mean go to sleep, but to enjoy being me. I have not had to look over my shoulder, and think about what other people think of me and in turn worry that I should just try to please all. It is for people to just take me for who I am; I find that it is a shame that 'the agony within', can be such a destructive thing.

One great saying that my work colleague told me is:

"Life is not a rehearsal"

This is so true, you only get one shot at this life. With this in mind, I find it quite fascinating that there are so many people who are suffering out there, which transpires when I talk about what I have experienced and people start to tell me how they feel. This could be good or bad, but it is just the way that they are, at that moment in time. A few people that I have spoken to, seem to want to talk about it. It is as if there is no one out there to listen to them. For me I do not go out of my way to tell them my story but it just seems to come out. Do I feel good after telling them? To be honest, yes I do. What do I have to be ashamed of? This was something that happened that was outside of my control.

I spoke to my boss in general, with regard to my breakdown. He said it was not and it was just a blip. After thinking what he said, this has been a long blip, but I just did not see it coming. I think a lot of people are going through the same thing but do not know what to do. Something that I did not realise is that my daughters are so protective and I realise that they do not want me to go back to those days. Yes I enjoy work still and yes it is a big part in my life, but not as big as my family. I think before the breakdown, it may well have been the other way around.

When I have openly spoken to people at work, since we have been producing this book from my notes, and I have discussed my illness, I am surprised by the amount of people that have or thought that they have suffered depression, anxiety, and even a breakdown. I do believe that these people suffer in silence. Just to talk about their experiences may have just given them some sort of relief. I can hear it in their voices. They start to talk and although I am not a doctor, I do have an insight into how 'the agony within' can affect your life. What it has shown me is that this condition appears to affect more people than we imagine. I really do believe that we need to do more for people who are suffering in this manner. Could the answer lay in the need to raise awareness? How many children does this condition affect? What they experience they take into their adult life and this then could destroy them. I know that destroy sounds exaggerated but until you have been through 'the agony within' you just do not know the impact. I believe that we should talk about it more and not make it sound like a disease, which should be pushed under the table. However one of the words that made me both smile and cry is *breakdown.* It is not as if I am a car that you can put in a garage and come out fixed in a few days. For some people this can take years and destroys marriages, lives and jobs. So the more we can do to remove the stigma that goes with what I call 'the agony within' then the better for all of us.

Chapter Nineteen: Family

If I had to put into words, how I feel about my wife Debra, my daughters Rosie and Roberta, together with my mum and dad; then it would be this.

When I find myself in the dark,
Your light will always spark,
For your love to me is so strong,
And to only me, do you belong.

I admire everything, for which you stand,
And would always take your hand,
For we have been together for some time,
And after everything you're still mine.

When we're together I feel your ache,
But my love for you, time cannot take,
Things might change, but not my view,
For me, I know it is still you.

I admire you and everything you believe,
For me whatever happens I will not leave,
Through life's troubles, I will remember you,
We're bound, by what we've been through.

'Family' created by Julia Everitt for Thomas Westmoreland.

The Agony Within